© THE BAKER & TAYLOR CO.

Going on an Airplane

FIRST EXPERIENCES

Going on an Airplane

BY FRED ROGERS

photographs by Jim Judkis

G. P. PUTNAM'S SONS
New York

With special thanks to: Nan Earl Newell;
Margaret B. McFarland, Ph.D., Senior Consultant;
Barry N. Head; the Hendrickson family;
the Lau family; Susan Williams;
the staff and the management of U.S. Air
and Pittsburgh International Airport;
and all the other families and friends
who helped us with the book.

Text and photographs copyright © 1989 by Family Communications Inc.
All rights reserved. Published simultaneously in Canada
Printed in the United States of America
Project director: Margy Whitmer
Book design by Kathleen Westray
Library of Congress Cataloging-in-Publication Data
Rogers, Fred.
Going on an airplane.
(A Mister Rogers, First experience book)
Summary: Details an airplane trip from packing
and arriving at the airport to the moment the
plane comes down to land in a new city.
1. Air travel—Juvenile literature. [1. Air travel
2. Airplanes] I. Judkis, Jim, ill. II. Title. III. Series:
Rogers, Fred. Mister Rogers' First experience book.
HE9787.R64 1989 388.7'42 88-30736
ISBN 0-399-21635-9
ISBN 0-399-21633-2 (pbk.)
First impression

Flying on an airplane is a unique adventure—no matter how many times we do it. There's something almost unbelievable about traveling up in the sky.

My mother was afraid of flying, so when my parents and I went on long trips, we went by train. I was a teenager before I first had a ride in an airplane, and I loved it so much that I learned how to pilot a plane by the time I graduated from high school. But just because my mother was afraid of flying didn't mean that I had to be. And learning to fly allowed me to see how carefully all pilots must check everything about a plane before they take it up in the air.

More and more children are traveling on commercial airlines these days—some with their parents and some (age 5 and older) without. Being familiar with the things to expect can be a great help in any new experience, and having the people you love show and tell you about those things can help all the more.

If your child is traveling without you, it's wise to talk with someone at the airline to find out its particular procedure for taking care of your child. Airlines are very specific about their care of young passengers. They consider them top priority for special care.

Helping children to know what they might expect in any first experience is one of the responsibilities and joys of being a parent. Encouraging your child to make whatever he or she can of any new adventure is one of a parent's greatest gifts.

—Fred Rogers

When you want to go somewhere far away, and you want to get there quickly, you might go by airplane. Airplanes travel a lot faster than cars, buses, or trains.

There are things you might like to take along to play with on the plane—like toys, books, crayons, or maybe a stuffed animal. You can pack them in a small bag.

You may also need to pack a suitcase with clothes and other things you'll want to have while you're away. Going away takes a lot of getting ready, but your favorite grown-ups will help you with all that.

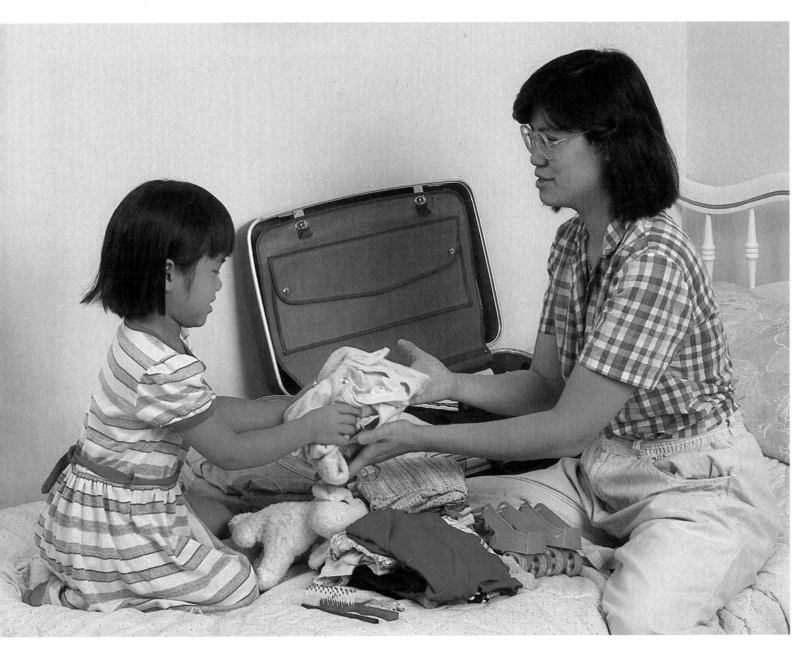

Airports are places where people go to get on and off airplanes. Airports are busy places! People with suitcases in all shapes and sizes. People coming and going in cars and buses and taxis. It seems as if everyone is in a hurry to get somewhere.

One of the first things you do at the airport when you're going to take a trip is check in with someone who knows where you need to go to find the right airplane. That person will look at your ticket and make sure that your suitcases get on the same plane as you do.

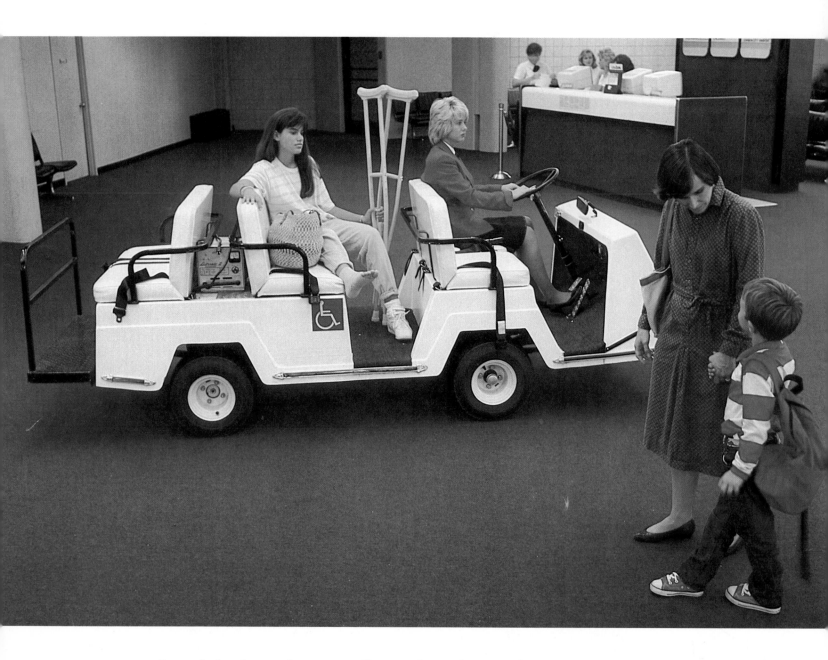

It might be a long walk to the place where you get on your airplane. People with special needs can ride in *carts* that make a beeping noise to let you know they're coming.

On your way, you may see restaurants, stores, and bathrooms.

Everyone has to pass through a place called *security*. The airport people will ask to see your little bag or anything else you're carrying. They will also ask everyone to walk one at a time through a special doorway. That way, they can make sure everyone is taking only safe things on the airplane.

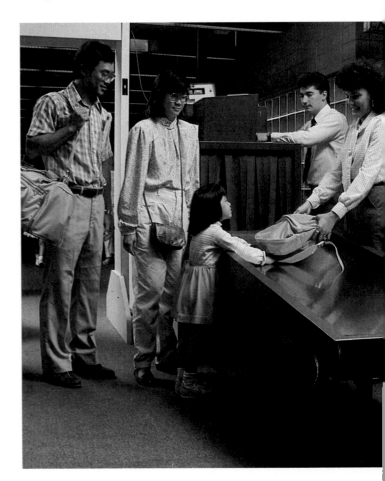

Then it will be time to find the right place to sit and wait until your airplane is ready for you to get on board. At the airport, those places are called *gates*.

Lots of families travel together, but some older children travel by themselves. The people who work at the airport and the people who work on the airplanes take special care of those children—so that they never have to feel as if they're all alone.

When it's time to get on the airplane, you might walk down a hallway called a *jetway*. At the end of that jetway, your plane will be waiting for you—along with the flight attendants who will take care of you during your trip.

When you're boarding your plane, you might see into the *cockpit*.
That's where the *pilot* and *co-pilot* sit as they fly the airplane.

Some of the things in the cockpit are like things in a car. Every airplane has a *steering wheel* and *brakes*. It also has a lot of *dials* and *instruments* that tell the pilot and co-pilot what they need to know—like how much fuel the airplane has and which way to go even when the airplane's in the clouds.

Every person has a *seat* on the airplane, and the flight attendants will help you find yours. Flight attendants can't sit right beside children who are flying alone, but they're always nearby.

They'll show you where you can put your things, and they'll find you a pillow and blanket if you ask for them. Flight attendants try hard to help everyone feel comfortable.

In fact, above each seat there are *buttons* for cool air, for light and for calling a flight attendant if you need help.

It's just as important to wear a *seat belt* in an airplane as it is in a car. Airplane rides can sometimes be bumpy. Flight attendants know how the seat belt works, and they know about other things to keep you safe.

When the plane is ready for *takeoff,* all the passengers will be in their seats with their seat belts on—even the flight attendants.

Then the plane will move down the *runway,* going faster and faster, until all of a sudden it will start to go up in the air. In a moment you'll hear the sound of the airplane's wheels folding up out of the way.

The plane will go higher and higher until you are way up above the place you've left behind. If you get a strange feeling inside your ears, swallowing hard a few times can usually make that feeling go away.

Some people like to look out the window while they're flying or use the special tray in front of them as a table for drawing and coloring.

The flight attendants might give you a snack or even a breakfast or lunch or dinner while you're up in the air. They'll certainly bring you something to drink.

They get the food ready in a small kitchen called the *galley*. They don't usually cook there, but they do get things ready to serve to everyone on the plane. They work fast!

It's best to stay in your seat as much as you can. You'll be safer, and anyway, there isn't much room to walk around.

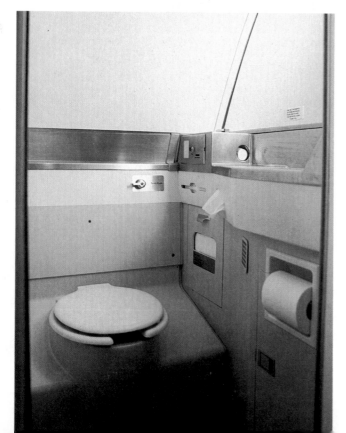

People can get up to go to the bathroom, though. The bathroom is usually in the front or back of the plane.

It's very small, but it does have a sink and a toilet. The water from the sink and what you flush from the toilet goes into a big tank inside the plane. When the plane gets to another airport, special machines clean out that tank.

As the plane is about to land, you'll probably hear the sound of the wheels folding down again. That means you'll be back on the ground soon—at another airport in a different city!

If you're traveling with the people in your family, you'll be on your way with them. If you're traveling by yourself, you'll stay with a flight attendant or someone from the airline company until you are with the people who are expecting you at the airport.

An airplane trip is a real adventure, but all along the way there will be grown-ups to take care of you. They know how exciting traveling can be, and they'll give you all the help you need until you're safely back home again.